Praise for Jacob Shores-Argüello

"'When my mother died, I was without boundary,' writes Jacob Shores-Argüello in this deeply personal and insightfully political book. Grieving for the loss of his mother and the loss brought on by capitalism, colonialism, and climate change, Shores-Argüello maps a transnational Latinx experience from Costa Rica to Oklahoma while connecting to Indigenous communities and activism globally. This encompassing and compassionate poetics—one in which the poet finds 'everything is citizen around me'—poignantly urges us to retune our senses and re-embrace our world in all its interconnected wonder."

—BRANDON SOM, author of *Tripas*

"This book dissolves all borders—of nation and self, human and animal, form and language, memory and make-believe. We enter this book searching, searching for home, and in the end, the only home to find, the only one we ever had, is migration itself, change itself. This book is shockingly wise, funny, and full of mourning—a wake for our delusions. Jacob Shores-Argüello is a true original."

—REBECCA GAYLE HOWELL, translator of *The Belly of the Whale*

"In *Grief for the Green That Was,* Jacob Shores-Argüello sings a poignant elegy / eulogy // elogio / elegía, yet witnesses the slow growth of naïveté into new life: glasswing butterflies become citizen pollinators, a river in New Zealand earns personhood. Amid rivers of fog and forests of cloud, beneath skies the color of rum, among hillsides bejeweled by coffee cherries bright as rubies, the speaker transforms himself into a citizen of grief, un huérfano // vidente / ciudadano de este mundo y del siguiente."

—DIEGO BÁEZ, author of *Yaguareté White*

"In his formally adventurous and bold *Grief for the Green That Was*, Jacob Shores-Argüello shows us that he is a poet of place who interrogates the distance between home and our memory of it. But nostalgia is not his mode; rather, longing is, a longing for what time inevitably destroys."

—TOMÁS Q. MORIN, author of *My Favorite Things*

"The Pan-American Highway connects a once rural coffee-growing town in Costa Rica with a small city in the plains of Oklahoma. *Grief for the Green That Was* is a family story between these two points, with migration as the headwater from which these river-poems flow, and memory the landing place for umbilical climates and personal grief."

—G. A. CHAVES, author of *Wallau*

"*Grief for the Green That Was* is a spellbinding testament to what remains when memory becomes an act of survival. Jacob's poems shimmer with beauty, hard-earned wisdom, and a palpable desire to understand the hows and whys of 'Mother grief, motherland grief': a sorrow that lives in the body, across oceans, here and there. They insist that even in the most vulnerable places—an eroding riverbank, a hospital café, a family cemetery—something stubborn and green still grows."

—MARCUS WICKER, author of *DEAR MOTHERSHIP* and *Silencer*

Grief for the Green That Was

Camino del Sol

A Latinx Literary Series

Rigoberto González, Series Editor

Jacob Shores-Argüello

Grief *for the* Green That Was

TUCSON

The University of Arizona Press
www.uapress.arizona.edu

We respectfully acknowledge the University of Arizona is on the land and territories of Indigenous peoples. Today, Arizona is home to twenty-two federally recognized tribes, with Tucson being home to the O'odham and the Yaqui. The university strives to build sustainable relationships with sovereign Native Nations and Indigenous communities through education offerings, partnerships, and community service.

ISBN-13: 978-0-8165-5628-1 (paperback)
ISBN-13: 978-0-8165-5629-8 (ebook)

Cover design by Leigh McDonald
Cover photograph of banyan tree roots by wissot/AdobeStock
Designed and typeset by Leigh McDonald in Granjon LT Std 10.5/14

Publication of this book is made possible in part by the proceeds of a permanent endowment created with the assistance of a Challenge Grant from the National Endowment for the Humanities, a federal agency.

Library of Congress Cataloging-in-Publication Data
Names: Shores-Argüello, Jacob author
Title: Grief for the green that was / Jacob Shores-Argüello.
Other titles: Camino del sol
Description: Tucson : University of Arizona Press, 2026. | Series: Camino del sol: a Latinx literary series
Identifiers: LCCN 2025045438 (print) | LCCN 2025045439 (ebook) | ISBN 9780816556281 paperback | ISBN 9780816556298 ebook
Subjects: LCSH: Shores-Argüello, Jacob | Grief—Poetry | Loss (Psychology)—Poetry | Climatic changes—Poetry | LCGFT: Autobiographies | Autobiographical poetry
Classification: LCC PS3619.H6657 G75 2026 (print) | LCC PS3619.H6657 (ebook)
LC record available at https://lccn.loc.gov/2025045438
LC ebook record available at https://lccn.loc.gov/2025045439

Printed in the United States of America
♾ This paper meets the requirements of ANSI/NISO Z39.48-1992 (Permanence of Paper).

Los Pollitos Dicen

Los pollitos dicen
Pío, pío, pío
Cuando tienen hambre
Cuando tienen frío

—NURSERY RHYME

Contents

Foreword

"Verde que te quiero verde" is arguably one of Federico García Lorca's most well-known lines. "Green how I want you green," from "Romance sonámbulo"—a poem that situates the color within the familiar space of nature but on a landscape intimate with life and death, imbued with the seductive power of beauty and the dizzying melancholy for that which has been lost, forbidden, or perpetually out of reach. How fitting, then, that the title of Jacob Shores-Argüello's book highlights the charge of that color, which also represents the ancestral homeland: "Back in my mother's Costa Rica of green."

The speaker of *Grief for the Green That Was* returns to Costa Rica feeling unmoored, the distance from his earlier memories, from his Tico identity, growing further as he comes to terms with the death of his mother and with the potential loss of his Costa Rican citizenship. Additionally, like all rainforested countries of the Americas, Costa Rica has become vulnerable to climate change and is under constant assault by the greedy entitlements of urbanization and tourism. *Change* is another word for *loss*.

Confronted with this amalgamation of dramatic changes, "Mother grief, motherland grief," the speaker begins to gather memories and experiences located in other places that trigger emotional associations, such as Oklahoma—his father's homeland—where the speaker and his mother also lived and loved. Bridging Oklahoma to Costa Rica is an act of repairing the fragmented:

> If you look at I-35 on a map
> you'll realize it was always the Pan-
> American highway. It rides
> right by my grandmother's house
> in Oklahoma. It rides right by my

grandmother's house in Costa Rica,
where the old men talk about
the time when tortillas
never saw a microwave.

And to achieve a moment that approximates closure, a restorative pause in the journey after he suffers yet another personal loss, the speaker concludes the story of his parents' marriage with a heartbreaking gesture:

My father's last move was when I brought
his ashes back to my mother's grave.

Neither the journey nor the story concludes for the speaker, however, who takes a trip to New Zealand, where he finds the familiar afflictions of commercialization and global warming but also signs of hope, like "Whanganui, the first river in the world to be granted legal personhood" to secure its preservation. Inevitably, the natural landscape transports him back to Costa Rica, which brings both comfort and sorrow. This section of the book, modeled after "choose your own adventure" books, in which the reader assumes the protagonist role, making decisions that affect the main character's fate, speaks to the unpredictability of the days ahead but also to a willingness to follow different paths and a receptiveness to new memories and relationships. This widening of the speaker's view of the world allows him to navigate that overwhelming emotional state ("without / my mother, / I am a citizen / only of grief") that had once seemed incurably repressive and isolating.

Shores-Argüello writes so compellingly about loss that it feels unjust or unkind to say that this book is our gain because it offers solace and direction in a time of distress and destruction. Above all, he reminds us of one of the most bittersweet truths in our humanity: that when we experience grief, we also experience love.

—Rigoberto González

Grief for the Green That Was

The *Change* in Climate Change

My cousin Santi WhatsApps from Costa Rica, fits the family
into the rectangle of video as they wave from the balcony.

He turns the phone, shows me a swirl of birds in the hurting sky.
But they are not birds. They are neighbor Tinoco's roof tiles

flying in a storm's rotary energy. My family is calling because
I'm in Oklahoma, which, to them, is a synonym for tornado.

My cousin lowers the phone for our grandmother to hear.
She's scared because she's lived in the town for eighty years

and can't recognize all these new skies. Because a year before,
a hurricane reaved its way across this country for the first time

in recorded history. Tornado or torbellino or something else,
I ask her about the valley's strange wind. And she laughs, says

that she was calling to ask me the same thing. I don't know why
I keep forgetting the *change* in climate change. My grandmother

sighs as the sky darkens to the color of rum. Why I still think
that we'll have names for all the things that will come.

I.

Los Pollitos Dicen

(First Person)

The farm my mother left me grew nothing but clouds. It was at the very top of a mountain, and when the clouds cleared you could make out a flea-sized white speck: the rambling basilica in the far below, kick-drum heart of the country, where the water was Mary-touched and bottled for the sick. But the clouds never cleared. On the top of the mountain, you never knew if you were the thing living closest to, or farthest from, God.

The farm was a sloping green covered in gnarled trees. Trees that pulled water from clouds, water that made streams, streams that made rivers for the valley below. More than any tourist beach or palm tree, this was the Costa Rica of my family's imagination.

• • •

A calf was missing, my cousin Santi said. He'd gone looking for it, but with no luck.

I told Santi I wasn't worried. The calves had been born around the time when my mother had died, when none of the family'd had time to check in on them, and so they were wilder than any animals we'd ever had. Sometimes they didn't come for their feed; sometimes they'd let you look and look, call and call, and nothing. And just when you put them down as dead, frozen solid, or fallen off some terrible cliff, they'd come ambling out of a cloud to chew on some grass at your feet. Little bored Lazaruses, caring nothing about your worry, their eyes blinking, huge lashes opening and closing like moths. Still, the calves were worth a lot of money, and Santi was right to have given a good long look.

We'd come to the farm soon after my mother died, so Santi could tend the cattle, calm them with ear-spooned coos before he gave them their monthly injections. Santi's father had gifted us a bottle of rum to last our few days on the mountain. "To keep you two warm," he'd said. That night, we lifted small glasses of self-perpetuating rum, flower after flower. We got out the cards and worked the rabbit ears of our old TV. After a few games, a few bueno pero no te enojes, a few drinks, Santi got it in his head to go looking for the calf again.

We walked into the saturated night, mud and seedlings beneath our feet. Our flashlights reached a few meters, enough for us to see a bit of the cloud-forest trail but not enough to walk confidently. I let my light wander onto snaking vines, huge umbrella-sized leaves, delicate fern work.

Yes, my mother had died, but everything else was just as it had always been.

Until it wasn't. There, in a curve of the trail, I thought I saw something in the mist. I narrowed my eyes and could just make out an animal-like shape. A big animal. I pointed a finger.

"What, you see the calf?" Santi asked.

"Just look," I whispered.

The shake in Santi's voice. "I think . . . I think that's a . . . pantera."

Then it was gone.

• • •

We ran back. Out of danger, we started laughing, smiling. The joy of being both alive and more than alive. Fear waned. Wonder waxed. We couldn't let the panther we saw just be a panther. Santi swallowed more rum and stared at the full moon, declared we'd seen a moon panther.

"No, no," I said, "a ghost panther."

The ghost panther must have dragged our little calf away, Santi said. That was his great plot point. What if it wasn't dead yet? What if it was out there afraid and alone?

We went to a neighbor's farm, hoping to tell him about the panther, but no one was there. Instead, we found a small cage of yellow chicks chirping on his porch. The little chicks seemed to be saying something to me, but I didn't know what. I poked a finger into the cage, hoping to touch just one. I reveled in their velvet down, my childhood there with me.

Santi went out to raid one of our neighbor's chiverres, so huge he could barely carry it with two hands. He gave it to me and had me climb a hill so I could toss the gourd at him. On the slope, a patch of hortensias, the flowers that the family picks in times of mourning. I closed my eyes, and out there in the cloud forest it was funeral again, funeral everywhere. This worrying of memory, that's what I did with the impossible.

When I tossed the gourd, Santi macheted it with a single stroke before it could brain him. Strength: That's the way Santi deals with impossible things. He grounds himself in his body, builds trust in his own muscle.

Then Santi took off, marching with certainty, a deliberate speed. I rushed to keep up, sweeping the flashlight back and forth as we charged through a cloud. Two bodies moving fast. Bell bugs again, big leaves again, ferns again. And finally, that same panthery part of the trail again.

We stopped. Spotlight to the left, spotlight to the right. There in my flashlight's beam, as clear as any truth that I'd ever seen, I saw light reflecting in two perfect eyes, glowing circles floating in a cutthroat night.

"Ghost panther," Santi whispered.

No tree stump had eyes like that, no dog, no lost calf. No mistaking.

The cat's eyes just shimmered. Moon panther. The eyes looked deeply into me, casually explored all of my unseen parts. Nothing in my life had ever known me that way. There was a high-pitched moan, and I couldn't tell if it came from my mouth or the panther's. After the sound, the two eyes dissolved into the dark, impossibly gone. Ghost panther.

I jumped up and ran. Slipping on mud, I made it five steps before two new eyes appeared out of the nothingness in front of me. A new panther, the same panther, cutting off my escape.

I fell to my knees. I'd wanted this moon panther into being. I'd needed this toothy spirit to come and find me. I was desperate for it. Because if this ghost panther existed, then my mother could still exist too, somewhere in the afterlight.

It was coming for me because I'd asked it to come. In the dark of my mother's farm, I decided that if I had to die to prove the unprovable, that the border between this world and another was tissue thin, well, then, I'd die.

"Yes," I said to the panther as my cousin tried desperately to pull me up out of the mud.

"Yes," to the spirit, to the devil about to devour me. "Yes."

But on top of the mountain you never know if you are the thing living closest to, or farthest away from, God. I held my breath and presented my throat. The eyes would not move toward me. I lay there and wept. I was begging now. "Come for me, come for me please."

That's when it happened. No ghost panther, no moon panther, but the blinking on of a dozen other fireflies. All of them hovering, shimmering in the suddenly mortal night.

II.

Pío, Pío, Pío

(First Person)

Two Years Later

Back in my mother's Costa Rica of green

and cars and streets. Our shoes still clubbed in the closet,
her bathroom still with that whiff of sewer smell.

My bathroom, I keep forgetting. My house now.
I shower, and the mountain in the distance is beautiful

and is not enough. I'm back because my cédula
is expiring. My cédula is expiring because my mother

has died. *Expire*, what a mean and wiry word.
Drinking coffee at the kitchen table, I read an article

about the little town one town over, where the mayor
is giving citizenship to pollinators. Bees and trees

as fellow citizens in this time of climate change.
It's a beautiful thing to read. Outside, the trees are shaking

hands with each other; butterflies are claiming
their own little patch of living.

I walk outside and say hello to one of them,
hold out a single finger.

There is a kind of poem where this butterfly alights
between the first and second knuckle, showing

siblinghood, showing celebration and return.
This butterfly gaining its citizenship just as I am

losing mine. But this is not that kind of poem.
I keep on walking until a cut of red against the sky

comes down as a flock of macaws, full of chatter
and squawk. When the butterfly finally does loop by,

it doesn't notice these birds. The giant glasswing,
full of light, ignores the trees, the bees,

and me, so beautifully, as is its right.

Quicksand

I cup my hands in the barely moving
current of the river behind my house
until a chill reddens my fingers.
It tastes perfect, water's idea of water.
The river used to splay so beautifully
but now it's dying. I think about when
I was young, when there were so many
television shows with quicksand in them,
as if quicksand were this constant threat.
I understand it now, this need to overcome
things that are impossible to hold on to.
After I cross the river, I turn to drink again.
But as my mouth gets close, I remember
that everything is citizen around me, and I
talk to the water instead. I speak about
my mother, about the river's own sickness.
The river is changing, yes. But I hope,
for its sake, that it can change slowly.
A minor comfort, the best I can imagine
for both of our bodies. River, we've reached
the age where we know it's the quick,
and not the sand, that'll kill you.

Not Yet

The river behind my mother's house
used to be a river. Not anymore, not since
the nearby city bullied in, redirected,
and buried all but a shallow, watery lash.
Made worse by these long days of drought.
A river vulnerable, a river at risk. Impossible,
I once thought, that you could threaten
a river like that. Of course, as a kid of the eighties,
I already knew you could pollute;
that was, after all, how acid rain and Ninja
Turtles were made. But this diminutization,
this humiliation, was different. Back then,
when people from the States would come,
they didn't stay long, because my family
lives in a place where people live
and not in the places where tourists go.
Our trips were to the coffee-processing plant,
then to the water treatment plant.
These were the family prides: clean water
that the neighboring city would draw,
coffee that the world would claw at.
There is something important about
spending time with water and coffee,
coffee and water. But it never took more
than a day before the visitors would go
in clean white minibuses, only coming back
on their way to the airport. Stopping by
to tell me and my cousin about the wild beaches
they'd seen, the heaven-licking canopies—
this strange intimacy with a country
we thought was ours. These were people
who were plainly able. People who owned
owning. One of them told us rapturously

how she swam in an underwater cave,
and my cousin looked at me like we'd
become extras in our own movie.
Tourism is important, the radio always says.
But can currency mean more than a cédula,
a tarjeta de residencia, more than citizenship?
The river behind my mother's house *is* a river.
Dear River, I'm sorry to have robbed you,
in this poem, of your wild and only self.
Your inheritance, so deep and green.

Midair

Out at Ojo de Agua,
a thin girl jumps fully clothed
into her first water of the season.
Her tight school braids detonate
in the pool. Later, she comes back
in a swimsuit and climbs up
the diving board, the true
kink of her hair behind her.

It's been so long since
my mother died,
since anyone has warned me
against any kind of danger,
since I've been called Pío,
her gentle nickname for me.
I expected the ravages
of a death but not the loss
of these smaller tethers.

The diver makes it to
the highest point, and I find
myself wanting to learn from her.
How she owns three-dimensional
space, how she hurdles so beautifully.
I'm afraid I will never understand
myself again. Not in midair,
not anywhere.

Ghost Story

As a boy I pleaded
with the river to teach me
its long and winding vowels.
In exchange I taught it
swear words, how to play games.
The night I stayed by its side
for hours, eight parrots
came to listen to us speak.
It was a long time before
the river asked in a low voice
if the children of the pueblo
had finally forgotten La Llorona—
the woman who drowned
her children in its deep waters.
Yes, I said. Forgotten.
It's hard to lie to a river,
harder to lie to a river you love.

Grief, Grief, Goose

GRIEF

When my mother died, I was without boundary. The fence line of self, all burned up.
In her long last days, I took care of her. And in that time, whatever I was

was something
that spilled over. The hospice nurse, José Arturo, told me how this can happen.

Don't keep losing yourself to dying, he said.
If you do, you won't be there when the real death comes.

He was right, of course. The moment she died, I looked down
and couldn't tell if I was pushing away the hospital floor

or if it was holding me up. Grief, in its infancy,
is a hallucinogen.

GRIEF

It rained at the funeral and the air was cool and I had questions,
and *why* was one of them.

It was a philosophical question.
But I also had practical ones: How

do you walk away from a cemetery? How do you *just do that*?
I couldn't cry. I was too busy asking my *hows*.

How do you survive this whiplash grief, how do you keep driving
this thing called body?

GOOSE

I took a shortcut after my mother's funeral, downhill,
through the coffee bushes that were still alive in the valley

of fresh concrete and car fumes coming in from the capital.
Coffee is red fruit that clutches to its little bit of soil.

Very good coffee is shaded by trees that protect
the smaller plant from the sun's obsession.

On that funeral day, I found myself in that field. And the trees
were glazed with near rain, and I felt safe enough

to break down. Walmart owns that lot now.
I'm too tired to think about that anymore.

Just know that the land was rich. And now there is no shade tree left.
No coffee. When my mother died, I was without boundary,

but when this company crossed from North America
to Central, it caught me off guard.

This place where I first truly spoke to grief—
if you've invested in Walmart,

you've won it. I hope it is your treasure, a real choice,
and not some duck, duck, goose.

Because it used to be a place where you could be
alone and unalone all at once,

where you could finally cry
among the ruby fruit underneath the mothering trees.

Little Flower

On Fridays, the man
who cuts the cemetery grass
with his bent machete
takes his break early,
cradles up what sticks he can,
and trudges up the hill
of coffee plants.
Cemeteries and coffee fields,
the twin greens still holding on
in this town being smoothed
by trucked-in concrete.
As he leaves, I pass him,
grasshoppers erupting from
the low grass as I walk.
Adiós, we say to each other
as we meet, and I don't mention
that the man keeps hacking
at the flower I'm trying to grow.
Near us, the trucks are so
heavy with gypsum that they
test their weld seams.
This time, I don't go straight
to the grave but walk instead
to the river. A river that was
hurting even when I was young,
but now, with the climate,
is fully dying. Where will I go
when salvation dries up?
Today, I scoop a little cup.
My mother's grave is made
of the same concrete,

a big white box that
holds her, my father,
my cousin's mother,
our grandmother,
and our grandfather.
I bring the water to them.
Pour it gently on the little
flower and kneel in front
of almost everything
I have ever loved.

McDonald's

I didn't know what to say
back then, when the staff
at the hospital café
asked me about my day.
I wished I could have
pointed to my mother's X-rays,
let the cancerous lump
of moon speak for me.
But the staff were so used
to pain, they'd probably
just nod. If you want pity,
you need a civilian,
not this battalion
on the front lines of grief.
I went to the café
because it was not fast food.
Because my mother
was busy dying in her room.
And I was tired of North
American companies
buying up this place
I was suddenly
insisting was sacred.
That is what I told myself.
But really, I avoided
the McDonald's because
of the fryer alarm that my
limbic system kept insisting
was an ICU machine.
As a kid, all the movies
said that the battlefield
was where you got PTSD

A bullet and nothing less.
Certainly not a machinery
of beeps—this trigger I still
carry with me. To be honest,
I could work on it. I've seen
a doctor who has shown me
how to build a gentle wall
in my mind. But I don't.
I'm afraid that flashback
is all I have. That panic has
become the best part of me.
That pain is the way
I spell love.

Crossing Over

I.

After the funeral, I walk up the switch-
backs to the old mountain finca. And when
I finally arrive, your neighbor says
that he's recognized me from a distance,
not by the color of my shirt but from
the signature of my walk. That night
the bell bugs drop out of the night and thump
on their gorgeous thoraxes. I try to sleep
against the cold cabin wall. But cold isn't
what's keeping me from sleep. Growing up
between two countries has meant that I've
always had to travel to my dead. But now
I've been living in Costa Rica for months,
and the yawn inside of me is the size of ceremony.

II.

In the morning, I try to climb to
the peak of the cloud-cooled mountain.
I walk along the old ox trail
and the mud pulls my rubber boots down
with its murky suction. I can only go
so far because my neighbor has felled trees
to stop the four-wheelers from doing
their violent geometries. I try to push
into heaven and heaven pushes back.
But when I get home, my neighbor
tells me that he was keeping an eye on
where I was by the disturbance in
the canopy. To him I was the birds
launching themselves into the sky.

Living

My uncle convinces me to empty myself.
By this he means that I've drunk
too much. By this he means ranchar.
When I am done, my uncle says he wants
to spear meat for the fire. He believes
that we should eat fat and speak truths.

On the river's shoreline, I start a fire
with a little tube of red floor wax
as fuel. I stoke the flames and say,
under my breath, that no one would
notice if I died. I think that this is what
my uncle wants to talk to me about.
Instead, he says that his own children
don't speak to him anymore,
that no one would notice him either,
so what's left?

As a kind of answer, the river laps
near us with its muscly foam.
We hug each other as the hot fire
singes the little hairs on our shins.
We don't mention the kilometers
we had to drive to find this healthy
stretch of river. A river so alive,
it is our only definition of *alive*.

Back and Forth

The mountain's hem of concrete houses
takes on a full Pozuelo yellow
as the sun faints behind the clouds.
I am a child, but I have learned early
to avoid the rum in my uncle's Coke,
to be careful on the footbridge where
the bougainvillea are so thick that muggers
can hide. The house is filled with airline
magazines that I've had for months, snuck
into my backpack. My plan is to make
a goodbye collage for my mother out of
the glossy pages of black-and-white sky.
I don't know what is real. No grief yet.
This is the beginning of my sorrows.
And the pain of going back to Oklahoma,
to a cruel school, without my mother,
is just too much. On my last day, she makes
sure I have my favorites: lime mayonnaise
in the little cave of a split pejibaye, paletas
de coco, a pomegranate's sudden shrapnel.
"Pío," she says, "it's OK." Then she reconsiders:
"It *will* be OK." Getting onto the airplane,
I carry almost nothing in my backpack.
I have a flight attendant assigned to me.
In the seat, I soothe myself quietly by
thinking about my waiting father.
I try, really try, to grow up just a little more,
as I grow smaller and smaller.
As I fly like some meager migrating bird
into the future-colored sky.

Outside in Oklahoma

The family I'm staying with,
because my father is working,
have called their dog Darkness,
and it is a beautiful name.
I've decided to camp.
And out here in an old tent
on the edges of their property,
Darkness encircles me.
I burrow my back into the prairie,
strangely soft with a grass I don't
know the name of. I should know
the names of grasses, and of trees,
and of so many things.
                    Soon, the thick
wind loosens into coolness and the light
begins to dim. As I look up into Darkness,
the underside of her tongue is spotty
with inky-on-pink constellations.

Her body makes me think of my own body,
my fingertips dry as match heads
that will light this nameless grass if I'm
not careful.
            Darkness is a good teacher,
and she guides me to be gentle with myself.
With a nuzzle of her head into my hand,
she says, in her way, that I am OK.
I stroke her so long that the heavy night
settles, and all that is left is the white blaze
on her chest.
            Soon, my eyes, and I, will adjust.

But for now, I'm suspended
in this moment that is the sum
of all moments.
                                        The grass, it occurs to me,
is bluestem. The air is amniotic.
And I cry a good cry as the great dog
keeps on guarding me.

Oz

To steal a night with Oklahoma
I pitch a tent between two shallow ribs
of mounded dirt, the only windbreak
in this flat of land. In this country,
when night falls, it falls completely.
The stars *star* so loudly. Satellites make
unsubtle paths across the sky.

Out on the horizon, a lightning storm
starts popping off its flashbulbs.
It's a dangerous beauty, seeing what,
moments before, you could not see.

But my sky is clear, and so I sleep.
Until there is a flapping of plastic,
a nylon noise. My tent pole is torn
from its stake and finds my sleeping skull.
When the wind makes a balloon
out of my tent, the whole scene
is baggy and graceless.
Blown across prairie grass,
I'm pushed and pulled
by an everywhere of wind.

The day after the storm, the news anchors
on TV say *freak occurrence*, they say
once-in-a-century storm.
They say nothing about
the "once-in-a-century" that happened
two years before. How can something
be so big that you just don't see it?

In a bathroom mirror, I think only
about the bruise on my hairline.
I don't realize that my life has changed.
I don't realize that I've woken up
in another land completely.

Here or There

As a child, I wanted to find a way to delve into
astonishments. But in the backyard of a small Oklahoma
house there are few ways to have bigger wants. You can
look up and gaze at the sky until your neck hurts, but only
if you're willing to have the sun sit in your eyes for days.
My father says that this is the way it has always been in this town—
this longing to leave was the same when he was a boy.
My teacher tells me to stop *going on about it* when people ask
about my background. Just say *mixed*, as if families aren't
all a kind of mix. Then a boy knocks that word out of my mouth.
The Oklahoma paradox—a hit when "mixed" means too
different, a hit when "mixed" means daring to be too close
to him. And when that same teacher comes running, the boy
keeps telling her that I just lost my breath. *He just lost his breath.*
Later, on the phone, my mother and father talk about me
and this boy. They talk about her flying up. It occurs
to me that my teacher is right. My house is mixed—
here or there, there or here. The ache of leaving
mixed with the ache of having stayed.

Time Machine

In and out of small towns in Oklahoma
when I was young. Driving through now
for the first time in forever, and the shadows
on the highway from Paul's Valley
to Oklahoma City are lifeless with summer sun.
I stop at Braum's for some Neapolitan,
and the old men who are trying to make
a communal space out of the linoleum
still talk about the old "tamale" man
like he was Jesus.
Gentle talk is everywhere,
and all through the town someone
is loving someone else deeply.
Important, when the dust keeps
getting in your eyes.
If you look at I-35 on a map,
you'll realize it was always the Pan-
American highway. It rides
right by my grandmother's house
in Oklahoma. It rides right by my
grandmother's house in Costa Rica,
where the old men talk about
the time when tortillas
never saw a microwave.
In high school, both me and my mother
waited Oklahoma tables for $2.25
an hour plus tips. A bad shift meant
you ended up owing the bar more than you made.
Driving across the city limits,
I wonder, all these decades later, how much
they're paying now. Oklahoma City is
so built up now. This park is beautiful.

The downtown is full of restaurants
and basketball teams.
On my phone, I keep checking
and rechecking the restaurant minimum wage,
thinking I've got it wrong. But no, in 2023,
it's 3 dollars 63. I drive. I keep thinking.
About what jobs you need to afford nostalgia.
About 3.63. About how long a city wants
a person to work before they get to eat.

12. Behind You

1. Ten years since
I've worked
in a restaurant for ten years

2. Dish pits, bus tubs, and prep.
Kitchens sparking
with char and sweat.

3. After work
we'd try to drink a beer
for every table we'd served,
and we'd
sink,
sink.

4. *Well, at least you don't
have to take
your job home with you*,
a friend said.

5. But it's been ten years,
and in my dreams I'm still clocking
in late
for dinner shifts.

6. For slow Mondays, when you owe
the restaurant
more than you make.
For $2 and a quarter an hour.

7. I don't know what you see
when you die
in your sleep. But I think I'll be
in a crowded kitchen,
trying to get through.

8. *Behind you*, I'll say,
running my
trays.

9. *Behind you.*
Restaurants, the architecture
of my
anxieties

10. Because rent.
Because of running out of time.
Because of
making
due.

11. Because some jobs you just can't leave

In Oklahoma

The rumbling rust of a Ford Tempo—
speakers pushing air, we kids are the busted-

muffler lions of I-35, roaring down
the highway, yelling the same thing to each other

about the Oklahoma truck stops,
about the songs on our CD: *the next one, the next one*.

Here in gray and actual Oklahoma, we careen
down I-35, the same Pan-American highway,

the same umbilical, between North and South,
between Paul's Valley and San José.

Between our separated families, between our futures
and lasting pasts. We kids think only in norths

and souths. We have no *west* in us, as we try so hard
to grow up. As we, the future-starved flyers,

drive toward, or away, from the lives that our mothers
wanted for us, as we blaze by a MENUDO sign,

flashing half-broken: MEN, MEN, MEN.

Quietude

My dad was a big guy, and I
loved his large, hold-you-in-his-palm
hands. His loamy smell. A great
fatherly father. When he was young,
he worked with his hands in Alaska,
he pulled records in California. He mailed
boxes of pecans to who knows where
from who knows where. Then to
other places, to other farther away jobs.
Eventually, he met my mother,
who joined him, country to country,
for work together. After I was born,
she settled in his hometown while
he worked mostly away. When in Oklahoma,
he took good care of me, put himself
in between my mother and so many questions.
Questions they didn't ask about his
own moving body—as if maleness, whiteness,
made him worker to worksite and nothing more.
He retired with her, back to where she
was born. And when she died, we talked on
the phone, but he never talked much about
what happened. He didn't like to keep
turning over a thing. And now, I wonder,
if he wasn't right. What happened, what
happened—it's the work I can't put down,
the map I can't refold. My father's last
move was when I brought his ashes
to my mother's grave. I tried to do it
in a way that he would've liked
and tried not to say too much. At first,
the silence fit poorly, like a coat

I never grew into, but then I unmade
the careful masonry, opened up
the concrete mausoleum. And when I used
my hands to pour the ashes in, it felt right
when they swirled and fell quiet too.

Pacemaker

My father carried a heart
not entirely his—a pacemaker
that began to fizz one day,
sparking against his ribs.
I tried to lift him into a car,
and for a moment, electricity
passed between our bodies.
An inheritance of shock.
We looked at each other.
Not because it felt so strange
but because we *recognized* it.
Since the day my mother died—
this thump of voltage through
both our bodies, this thump
of our electric grief.

Paradise

I'm in this WhatsApp group,
where Ticos, some
in Costa Rica,
some in the USA,
talk about the Sele
and whatever else
is on TV.
And when someone
says that
The Simpsons are going
to Costa Rica,
the swell in the chat
gets nervous.
They try to predict
the jokes. Failing
infrastructure, rising violence,
huelgas,
or worse.
But when the show
finally comes on,
Marge says the word *paradise*,
and we all know
where this is going.
Someone in the chat
says it can be good.
Someone else says that desperate
needs always hide
desperate needs.
When the credits roll,
the joke is
to figure out
if there were any Costa Ricans
in the show at all.

The sloth? The monkey?
That waiter
who didn't speak?
The Simpsons
don't know it,
but this idea of Costa Rica
without people in it
is an old and dangerous
colonial logic:
first, you say it's empty,
then you say
it's yours.
After an hour,
there are memes
in Spanish
and in English.
Itchy and Scratchy at Palí,
Homero at every
local bar.
By the end of the day,
people are
putting themselves
into the cartoon.
I post nothing
as I think about
what that person meant
by "desperate needs."
As memes ¡Ja, ja!
As memes D'oh!
As people Photoshop
themselves
back into their
own homes.

Medical Migrants

My mother died of stomach cancer,
as did my grandmother and a cousin
who was my age. And I've not been able
to swallow properly for five months
and it's freaking me out. Not that I
am dying—it's not true that we are
always dying—but I do need tests.
This kind of cancer is a Costa Rican thing,
but USA insurance doesn't care about that.
So it's thousands of dollars, so it's them
saying it isn't "medically necessary."
My doctor argues with the insurance
that he's following Central American
guidelines. My doctor argues family history,
but insurance only has eyes for a standard
patient, and that standard patient is not me.
So now I am flying back to Costa Rica
to get things done, with $164 cash
in my pocket to pay the best doctor I know.
Me and all these wrapped up and hobbling
North Americans in the immigration line.
We, the broken bodies. Bodies whose
country cannot take care of us.
But, somehow, when bodies move north
these same people can't understand.
Some of my USA family were dust bowl kids
who traveled from Oklahoma to California
so they could feed themselves. My grandmother
could never understand how Oklahomans,
Oklahomans of all people, could have
a problem with people moving
to where they need to move.

When I was a kid at this same airport,
I didn't understand the hurting bodies.
The USA wants you to believe
that a foreign bullet is the thing that kills you.
And never says how a dollar can do the same.

Poem with Nineteen Footnotes in the Shape of Central America

I'm out in the Oklahoma panhandle,
and the unlikely 103°F forces me to think about
my breathing, about my past.[1] I'm back here
checking out the duplex[2] we lived in for a year,
but I don't remember much. That is, until
a beautiful man with a bandana on his head
walks across the road refusing to look at the sun.
What I recognize is this strange relationship
with the above. It never made sense why[3]
my mother's flight[4] was to Oklahoma[5] of all
places. I'm hungry and go out to the gas station,[6]
the only store around. I sit on the gravel
and look out. In the distance, the man has
had enough and shouts at the sun. I hurt for him.
This prairie feeling. We, the treeless,
we the aggrieved at our smothering star.

---

1. People say that smell is what makes a person remember. But for me, memory has always been triggered by sun or cloud.
2. I remember almost nothing about the duplex. Except for the little plastic pool that my parents put out in the front yard. I sat it in for hours. I remember asking my mother if we could put ice in it. Me, a little cocktail in the Oklahoma sun.
3. Of course, it was where my father was from. And it was the money they made, remittances sent to Costa Rica that put three generations into bloom.
4. When I was a kid, she read me the story of Icarus, and it all sounded good to me. And the lesson I heard wasn't "Don't be too proud" but "How can I afford all that wax?"
5. It's not like she hated it. She liked to drive into the city for the sales at TJ Maxx, and we'd bring back comforters and curtains for the house that her brother was promising to build her back home. Still, I inherited the idea that life was about going back to Costa Rica. She would retire there, my father would retire there. We would all, at one time or another, go back.[1]
    1. For good health care. The answer to everything is always good health care.

6. For a Hunt Brothers pizza. This chain secreted into gas stations across the USA that no one talks about. The largest pizza chain in the country. There was a time when the narrative was that the USA had everything, but there is so much sadness in this particular slice. Now, my Costa Rican cousins can walk to a gorgeous Indian restaurant[1] any time they want. So, sometimes new can be good.[2]
    1. But, of course, they don't actually go to the Indian restaurant. Too expensive. So many new things now, but most of it is for those with spare colones in their pocket. Or spare dollars, judging by all foreigners staying at the private hospital complex ringed by the nice restaurants.
    2. Nostalgia loves a second-generation kid. Me, in this strange Venn diagram with old Tico men who lament when the traffic backs up all the way to the old highway—*the way it was, the way it was*.[1]
        1. OK, it's a little more complicated[1] than that. Part of the Costa Rican founding lens is of a rural landscape, an agrarian democracy. And so a different kind of threat lives in the loss of rural spaces.
            1. I always think about the Statue of Liberty, how people can just drop that into a poem with no complication, no explanation at all. That just doesn't work with Juan Santamaría.[1] Efficiency[2] is hegemony's closest cousin.
                1. The national hero of Costa Rica. He is the one who drove the U.S. filibuster[1] William Walker out. The airport is named after him. The same airport that all the North Americans walk through.
                2. But maybe efficiency is not a kind of beauty?
                    1. A filibuster is a person who engages in unauthorized warfare.[1] In this case, with the intention of creating a slaveholding colony.
                        1. The war in question has roots in the Missouri Compromise. This law made the 36th parallel[1] the line that decided which states would come into the USA as slave owning and which would be free.
                            1. This parallel rides right across the top of Texas,[1] a place so devoted to slavery that they refused any land above it. Eventually Oklahoma took it over. The panhandle, this startling shape.
                                1. Of course, Costa Rica is below the 36th parallel too. So why not keep the terrible logic going? William Walker made himself the head of Nicaragua and stormed southward, trying

to make new slave states.
When he was beaten back, he
threw bodies into the wells
and cholera spread.[1]

1. Eventually, 10 percent of the Costa Rican population died.[1]

    1. Sitting on the gravel at a panhandle gas station, I shake my head. Strangers always laugh when I say I did my growing up in both Oklahoma and Costa Rica. As if one couldn't be tied to the other. As if the umbilical didn't exist. As if we didn't shape each other. As if the Americas aren't the Americas. As if Central America is just some small[1]

        1. footnote to the USA.

Writing Violence: I

I might be in Costa Rica, but I'm writing
for the United States, and so I wonder how
some people will hear it, with the small bones
in their ears sharpened by stereotype,
appetites so ready for blood that is not theirs.
I knew it, they'd say. Narcos, they'd guess.
And maybe they'd not be wrong, but how
telling that this is the Spanish that's made it
into their vocabulary. Or maybe it'll be
the opposite; they'll speak loudly to me
in brochures and vacations, tell me that,
in their opinion, violence has nothing to do
with Pura Vida. They'll bait me into saying hard
and sad truths that I'd hoped not to lift that day.
And after, I'll worry that I've said too much,
because I worry in a country where tourism
is currency, where dollars cut deep into
the riverbed. Don't say too much
or we won't fly down, and then where will your
little tourist buses go? This gag called paradise.

Writing Violence: II

I start to chorrear some coffee
in my mother's kitchen. And she
comes back home from the mall,
and sits on the couch, and runs her
fingers through her dog's fur.
She loves him so much.

"Pío," she says, "please." She is asking me
to draw warm water and heavy salts
for the ache that years of restaurants
and nursing have put into her feet.

Later, in the street between our house
and the mall, a woman will be grazed
by a stray bullet. She has a dog too.
And even later, I'll sit at my desk
and it will make me sick to put the detail
of the dog in, because I know that's
how you make some people care.

And even later, when I read this poem
at some library or another in the USA,
I will have to explain that, yes, there are malls
in Costa Rica. And I will hate the question
I'm always asked: "But this violence isn't

in the beaches or the rainforests, right?"
Which, to me, sounds just like: Tell me
it's not happening in tourist places.
Tell me it only happens
where people live.

Assimilation

Santi and I are watching poorly subtitled eighties TV,
taped straight off cable in the States and then packed

in my carry-on bag back to Costa Rica,
swapping out underwear and other supremely

unimportant things.
We are chewing through the fruit that hung low

on our backyard trees when I tell my cousin
how people in the States don't know that

oranges

are green. Maybe yellow. The color is about
the *inside* of the fruit.

You should see the grocery stores in the USA, how they gas
Central American fruit so they turn

orange,

I swear it Primo, so that not even
a centímetro of sweetness sneaks through.

My cousin laughs: They know you eat them, right?
You don't just look.

I bite into one of our little Romanesque arches
and smile when its unutterable

orangeness

replaces almost all of my brain.
But then TV, us cousins leaning in hard

for the USA commercials, for the few shows
with any people speaking Spanish in them. It happens so quickly

we don't even wonder if the TV is telling us wrong
when it says that we don't have enough, that we

aren't good enough, that Central American
is nowhere near American enough.

All those beautiful TV shows,
all those beautiful commercials.

All of it asking us to make
our own unmaking.

Two little boys caught off guard
by how strangely ashamed we are

of the glorious fruit in our bowls,
and suddenly wanting nothing more than an

orange
orange.

The Quiet Cousin

My cousin Luna still has her school skirt on, clutching
her big book of Ciencias with long-fingered hands. We are
young and she's trembling just outside our grandmother's house.
Because of all the yelling. Because of the arrival of her
sudden mother, a voice that none of us have heard in a long time.

I've been surprised for hours, waiting for her at the iron gate
with wide and searching eyes. It's plain that we should leave,
and it's plain that we shouldn't go too far.

We walk fifty meters to the old rust-trussed bridge.
Below us, a new pony walks by itself on the river's shoreline.
Brown mane cut like a toothbrush. When hoof meets stone
the pony sounds bigger somehow, otherwise we talk about it
like it's a child, like us. Somehow the young pony is enough
for my shy cousin to talk about it all for the first time.

On the bridge, she uses small words for big fears.
Jamás, I say. *No*. You are a treasure. All the family wants her.
It's not her fault that her mother had gone, and is apparently back,
from who knows where. Not your fault, not your fault, I repeat,
just as loud as the pony's clop.

My cousin tosses small waxy leaves down from the bridge,
watches them glint and float. She asks me to go through her
science book and translate into English beautiful names for the pony.

I flip through the book slowly and come up with *Habitat*, *Symmetry*,
Method. I feel like I am doing it wrong. But no, there's a stability
in the science that my cousin just loves. "A few more," she says,
"a few more before . . . ," but she doesn't say before what.

And so a pony named *Neuron*, a pony named *Hypothesis*,
named *Nimbostratus*, named *Biome* neighs and neighs as my quiet cousin
weighs what it means, and doesn't mean, to go back home.

Workshop

The pale sound of jilgueros trilling in the jungle.
Abuelo rocks in his chair and maps the birds
in his head, practiced in the geometry of sound.

My uncle stokes the cabin's black iron stove
with a short rod. The flames that come are his
loves. I cook—chile panameño, coconut milk—

a recipe I've wanted to try. Abuelo eats,
suppresses the color that builds in his cheek.
To him, the chile is a flash of snake in the mud.

He asks for plain rice, beans. Tío hugs his father,
kneels in front of the fire, whispers away the dying
of his little flames. We soak rice until

the water clouds. On the television, a fiesta . . .

The person I am showing the poem to
stops reading. He questions the TV,
circles it with a felt pen. "This feels so

out of place in a jungle to me. Can you
explain to the reader why it's there?"
For a moment, I can't believe.

You don't think we have 1930s technology?
The poem was trying to talk about stereotype,
gentleness instead of violence for once.

But now I should fill the little room
of my sonnet explaining how we own a TV?
A shame, because I had a great last line—

there was a parade in it, and a dancing
horse like you wouldn't believe.

III.

Cuando Tienen Hambre

(First Person)

Drought

All the family has moved into Costa Rica's citied valley,
away from the land. Still, I go out to the old farm
with my cousin Santi, drink coffee with our neighbor
who is still trying to pull céntimos out of the ground.
The neighbor talks about leaving, too. But he's afraid of where
he can afford to live. Afraid of the city. Afraid of how
South American supply connects to North American appetite
with an umbilical violence. We carry coffee outside
in thin metal cups. There is a farm a few countries
to the north where people run from climate, a farm
to the east where people have been forced to change
the relationship between their bodies and this world.
Here, our neighbor talks of little but the missing clouds.
He hands me his cup, kneels, and pulls up a small
proof of drought. A rootless root. Above me, the sky is
beautiful. Above me, the sky is a starving blue.

Citizenships

"Pollinators were the key," says Edgar Mora, reflecting on the decision to recognise every bee, bat, hummingbird and butterfly as a citizen of Curridabat during his 12-year spell as mayor.

—PATRICK GREENFIELD, *THE GUARDIAN*, "'SWEET CITY': THE COSTA RICA SUBURB THAT GAVE CITIZENSHIP TO BEES, PLANTS AND TREES"

I don't have to go
too far,
a few hours tops,
to get to Curri
if I go up the old
road. The same
route the pilgrims
take on their
yearly walk
to the basilica.

I don't have to
go too far
to find the Walmart,
the McDonald's,
a Denny's.
Before I find
all the development
where the old
and the new
highways meet.

I don't have to
go too far
before I see
the idea I read
about in the
newspaper,
to give
pollinators citizenship

to this town,
giving them
the rights to cross
this lash of city.
Rivers, mountains,
and green spaces
preserved for these
oldest citizens
to cross.

I don't have
to go too far before
a hummingbird
comes near me,
investigating
the trumpet
of a flower
growing out
of a crack of a
concrete bench.
I wonder out loud
if she knows
she is a citizen.
The small bird
banks and curves
around my head,
her thread of tongue
threatening to dip
into my ear.

I don't
have to go too far
before I
start thinking
that without
my mother,
I am a citizen
only of grief.

Arcadia

Back up the mother mountain
for the first time in a year.
When the jeep turns,
my body presses
into the metal door,
a conversation
spoken in centrifugal force.
There's a sliver
of me who believes
in things that cannot
be believed in.
The ghostly part of me.
And so I close my eyes.

When I open them,
the jeep is climbing.
How long has it been
since my uncle has turned
this same turn and driven
off this same cliff?
And here I thought my mother
would be the family's
only death.

In Oklahoma, I dreamed
of living in this cloud forest,
heaven this family cabin on top
of a milky hill. In Oklahoma,
under the heat and hate
of children, I dreamed.
But I forgot
to dream of dying.

We hard turn into a curve,
and when the jeep stops, I walk
to the edge, out to a strangle
of trees that are just now healing
themselves. I kneel at the car-sized
hole that my uncle has left
in this world.

The family question is
whether he had his heart attack
and then drove off the cliff
or if it was the cliff that did it.

It's hard to believe that the
difference matters. Slippage, yawn,
the rocky beyond beneath you.
But it does.

Olla de Carne

It's a riddle. What's a cloud forest
without clouds? What's the river
below without anything to feed it?
Here on the dormant volcano
above our town, we cousins
talk about the end of the world.
We arrange the bones to spell
out things to heaven, although
we've forgotten which way heaven is.
There's only drought rock
and fugitive thorn in the undergrass.
We do eat, curled over our bowls.
We do drink; it's not that bad.
But how long can a river, can
a family, last without rain?
We yell at a host of angels, ask them
to drag water down from heaven.
When nothing happens, we rely on ritual
and dip back into our soup.
A spoonful of ritual, liters of ritual,
a stormless storm of ritual
the last best thing we have.

Far from Home

In this surprisingly dry country,
the evidence of my fingerprints
is on everything. An untrustable
dust follows me, gives away where
I've been. Santi has brought his
brindled boxer up the mountain,
the puppy of my mother's dog,
now grown. On my walk with her,
there are thorny inedible plants
that I've never seen before. *Well,*
this climate is good for something.
It's a small joke just for the dog.
I want to ask her what she remembers
of my mother, of this mountain
when it was still inside the clouds.
But I don't know if it's OK to speak
of grief to an innocent dog.
Mother grief, motherland grief.
Grief for the green that was.
Instead, I tell her that we
are heading back, and her tongue
hangs with such happiness.
But back where? How do you go back
when it's your home that's changing?
When it's your home that's
far from home.

After the Rain I

Little foams of frog spawn float in the new
water, stirring up an unearthly gloss. I lean in
to clear a choke in the rocks with a shovel.
After some time, I manage to convince a season
of dead things to come through the seam.

The leaves rush, like they are looking
for some lover waiting in the valley below.
All this water will join other water, which will
make a river out of the clouds. I am out there
shaping the land so the naciente won't back up,
won't flow wide and threaten landslide.

This land is land that's always been wedded
to water, but after the long drought, it needs
help finding its memory of ruts and channels.

In the distance, the lights of the town mean
nothing—no road, no car can make it this far.
Not anymore. Soon, I will have to think
about how I will eat, how to stay warm
in this world of washed-out roads.

In the morning, I walk down to the neighbors
who have dug a cave out of the cliff wall.
They've turned it into a little store, offering
what they can. Lime-dusted plantain chips
and jars of homemade jelly sold to no one.
They invite me inside, boil water for eggs.

I want this to be ritual, to be a celebration
for the rain. But it's hard to ask for water
for such a long time only for it to come
as emergency. In the cave, the little jellies

stack up. Wordless, the three of us sit and eat
the eggs, expecting nothing, using our thumbs
to separate the whites from their flames.

After the Rain II

The boarded-up barn next to the finca
is tinseled with pig blood and gummy
streaks of resin. A cow has come
to steal the young shoots through the barbs.
Her milk pulls at her; the thorn
and wire snag on her coarse hide.
On the ridge, it is somehow midnight,
but here it is still light. The cow stays
yoked to her shadow, head down,
working cud, mouthing the words of her
remarkable language. I walk down to her,
making sure she isn't caught in the
bramble wire. She's not. She knows
too much to be hung up on simple things.
What do I do, alone with a heaving
mass of serenity? What do I tell her?
That it's rained? She knows that it's rained.
And so I am quiet, for once, as she lets
me stroke her, as she sends
the long muscle of her tongue
into the wild grasses.

With the Pollinators

I walk through lipstick coffee fruit,
out to where the old cars, left for parts,
are melting into the volcanic loam.
Alcohol erodes judgment,
and so I cease to measure the difference
between my body and what is not
my body. Just then, ribbons of bees
unspool from a tree. Just then,
swifts bite at the clouds.
I wonder if I should pee in this field.
I check if anyone's looking. No one is.
No one here, in this place forgotten
by humans. God bless, there's nothing
more beautiful than an emptiness
that's not empty. I'm unworried
for the first time in forever. I thank
a passing bird. I thank a tree.
I forget to pee.

Celebration After a Single Rain

I kneel by the river,
celebrating after a single rain.
Me, this guardian of grief,
this drug runner between
the living and the dead.
I speak to the river again.
Dear river with the long view,
I can see how to heal,
it's true. But please,
mineral beauty,
tell me how we both
stay healed.

IV.
Cuando Tienen Frío
(Second Person)

Later, when you marry, it is to someone whose life is split between two countries. Because who else would understand you. And so, years later, you find yourself in Aotearoa New Zealand. You like how they write it out like that, te reo Māori first and English second.

You are doing a special drive down the Whanganui River with Ruth, your spouse's aunt. You two are the only ones who want to do the drive, but for very different reasons. Ruth is behind the wheel the whole way because you aren't confident enough to drive on the wrong side of the road. Although you don't like how you think of it as the "wrong" side. You, the tourist now.

Auckland traffic is grippy. It's a city that loves to pull you—into construction, into a river of red brake lights. If you were in a hurry, you'd think that all this traffic was smothering, but you are in no hurry. And so you think that the city is simply pretty.

Pretty as you drive with Ruth up and over the hump of the gorgeous bridge. Pretty as you drive down toward the harbor full of skyscrapers.

You look out the window and all of it is new. Is this part of what being a tourist is? To look out a window and not see history? It's comfortable in a way that makes you queasy, like eating too much sugar when you are a child.

Ruth is independent, exacting, quirky, and mysterious. She's the first person you've met in this country, and you are tempted to think that the country itself is also independent, exacting, quirky, and mysterious. But you know too much to do something like that.

More than anything, Ruth is startlingly generous. Generous enough to pick you up from the airport the night before. Generous enough to drive you down to the river, to make a whole trip out of it.

The Whanganui, the first river in the world to be granted legal personhood.

You loop back across the city's Borgesian highways—knots of both slow and fast time. Then *through*, and, finally, *under*. One last long tunnel, and you are heading endlessly south. It's in that expanse of green that you realize you don't exactly know what you are doing.

You know that you've never given up the hope that you felt with those citizen pollinators in Costa Rica. And so you've been focusing on this river and its personhood from afar. And so you decide that you are driving toward *hope*. Then you laugh at yourself. You can't fathom what that could possibly mean.

You are glad you are with Ruth. She talks to you about her capacity for hope, explaining it all in a quick, almost throwaway line: "Sober for longer than you have been alive."

You've never spent time with someone who has so much of her life worked out, a confidence that has transferred into every detail of your trip.

Still, Ruth is careful to offer you some small choices. You hold onto these, because you still think that is what makes you you. But you like how little they are too. You like how, from time to time, your life becomes a sort of gentle "choose your own adventure," one where the ending has already been written out by a kind hand.

If you find comfort in this, turn the page.

But you don't want to find too much comfort in this. It's too easy for you. You don't want to turn Ruth into your mother. Or into some other impossible ideal. Marianismo shares its headwaters with machismo.

You talk about these concepts with Ruth. She talks about a Kiwi concept in return. She walks you through the idea of being a "tall poppy." How all her life she was told not to be too proud. Tall poppies are the ones that get their heads lopped off.

This reminiscence starts her talking about her own mother, how . . .

But she doesn't finish her sentence. Suddenly, there is a tire screech, and Ruth is swerving around an out-of-nowhere Audi. The seat belt bites into your neck.

After the swerve, Ruth announces that you're stopping at a McDonald's, like it's something you've both earned. It's not something you want to do, exactly, but not something you protest.

You stop at a corner franchise and pull hard on its glass door. The river of cold air rushes onto you, stinging the friction burn that the seat belt has left on your neck.

It is McDonald's air. Nothing more, nothing less. Same as in the USA. Same as in Costa Rica. Same as every McDonald's you've ever been to.

Ruth asks if you want an "NYC Benedict Bagel." A little choice to center you. A sandwich from the States so you can feel like you are at home.

Politely, you don't point out that the NYC Benedict Bagel is the only thing on the menu that you can't get in the United States.

Ruth is big on finding home. She's told you that it might be because she was adopted, the haze of her birth making her expert at finding family wherever she can.

Or maybe Ruth is careful not to tie her present so absolutely to her past. One of many things you can learn from her. Ruth, in her mid-sixties. Ruth, unapologetic.

You are thinking about how branched the river of your love for her has become. How quickly. That's when you realize that she's still looking at you, wondering if she shouldn't have trusted you with even this simple question.

Ruth is just waiting to order breakfast. And so, for the first time that day, you get to make your little decision.

If you want an NYC Benedict Bagel, turn to page 78.
If you don't want an NYC Benedict Bagel, turn to page 80.

You go back inside the restaurant and order a desperate coffee. The side of the coffee machine is laminated with a large picture of a river winding through a field of beautiful red coffee fruit on a rolling hill.

As you wait for your coffee, you lean over the counter so you can get a better look, trying to find any signature that this picture might be Costa Rica.

You are nearly tipping over the counter when an employee comes to ask you what you need. You try to explain, "Sorry . . . I thought I saw someone I knew."

Turn to page 81.

The sandwich tastes . . . like you guessed it would taste. You are deeply familiar with it, even though you've never had one. There must be some kind of value in this.

You look at the crescent moon your bite has made of the sandwich, the little river of grease that is running down your wrist. You leave the rest of it on its little paper wrapper.

Shit.

As you leave the McDonald's, you realize that you've forgotten your coffee. Do you go back for something so minor?

If there is no such thing as a minor coffee, turn back to page 77.
If you plow ahead nonetheless, like a river rolling over rocks, turn to page 81.

McDonald's is a mixed paper bag for you.

In Costa Rica, no North American who came to visit would want to go to McDonald's, because why would you? You don't travel that far just to go to a place that you've been to before. That's not what "good tourists" do.

But Costa Rica was the first country outside of North America to have a McDonald's. And so it's woven into the culture. It's part of the landscape. McDonald's next to a mountain, McDonald's where the river splits in two.

For years, the McDonald's downtown was one of the places that stayed open late in San José. Somehow, you've had greasy-fingered conversations with second shifters, with drunk bankers, with singers needing to give their vocal cords a break after their stint at the national theater. All these beautiful people missed by the tourist who says *no*, who prefer something that fits into their idea of the word *exotic*.

McDonald's is a company that crushes local foodways. McDonald's got a lot of love when that first restaurant closed down. More than one thing can be true.

You get back in the car and Ruth keeps driving toward the river. And the land turns spectacularly rural.

Occasionally, you drive through a town center. This means that there is a dairy, which is like a Costa Rican pulpería. There is a bakery for custard squares and sausage rolls. Sometimes there is some kind of restaurant. Fish-and-chips, noodle places. Takeaways with spectacular photos of chaats and dosas.

The Oklahoma part of you finds this strange, that there are people out here living in their town centers, instead of everything being shuttered or turned into antique stores.

You look around at all the life and wonder if this is what it was like in small-town Oklahoma for your USA grandmother. Before all the Walmarts and McDonald's restaurants came.

Ruth warns that you'll be driving into a thick fog. There is no choice. You don't know how she knows this, but nonetheless you believe.

Your mother's cancer has colored how you feel about driving into something you can't avoid.

But Ruth is a driver, and so she drives. The valley is wide. You can see the top of the cloudiness below you, and then, just like that . . .

. . . your little car is drifting in the middle of a river of fog.

Perhaps too easily, you find yourself transported back to your mother's cloud-thick farm. Back to a past that you've being trying to heal from. But this is the way it's always been with you. Bleed then scab. Scab then bleed.

Down in the valley, the temperature drops by several degrees. And you are cold with cold, and you are cold with grief.

But there is no panther here. The only animals around are comical and multiple, chatty and wholly wooly. Eventually Ruth stops for a sheep crossing that fully envelops her car. A living river of animal. You look at the gorgeous group of ruminants. The kind of animals that hold tight to each other for safety.

The sheep go on for so long that Ruth makes a joke about not counting them or you'll both fall asleep. She turns on the radio to pass the time. There is a comedian on telling jokes about needing a hearing aid at age forty-seven. It's deeply wise in a way that shakes you, briefly, out of your chilly grief. The woman on the radio makes the unstoppable river of time funny. You like this woman.

Then it turns serious. She is talking about feeling pushed away, degree by degree, from the workings of this world. She wishes the country were more bilingual. Te reo Māori in more schools, in more parts of the government, in the society as a whole.

She is talking about connection, even when she is not talking about connection.

When the last sheep passes, Ruth starts the car and begins moving carefully. She holds tight onto the steering wheel and leans two inches closer to the windshield, as if this minor distance can help her navigate the fog. When she finally drives into clear air, you can feel your body relax.

An hour later, Ruth leans in again, now trying to spy the tiny road she wants to turn on. You see a church in the distance—Victorian, remote, and cliff hung. You see a river behind it in the far below. The Whanganui in the far below.

But by the time you park, you realize that you are too high up. There is no way to get down to the river, and so you go into the church.

It has a large main room filled with dormitory-style beds—an old convent now used for lodging. You wonder if you are going to stay the night.

Ruth finally reveals. The reason you are here is because it's the place where a famous poet was buried. She walks you out the front door to a plastic pamphlet container with little maps.

This is her making you feel at home again. She says, why don't you go and look for him?

If you go look for him, turn to page 88.
If you wonder, why on earth, you would ever go look for him, turn to page 89.

HIDDEN POEM

If you've found this poem, it's because
you went off track. It's because you are
looking for the things you've hidden.
You've hidden how you've been falling
off your own bones. You've hidden
how cancer is a cell that divides. How
bad things can keep going and going,
not knowing where to stop until the whole
organism dies. How efficiency is not
the only kind of beauty. How a river
can split from itself just to remingle,
and there's no telling which was which.
How all your flights, all the back and forth
that has shaped you, how *damaging* it must
have been. To you, to the environment.
How there are little borders in your mind
that you don't cross. How a river is so often
a border. How a river is always a coming
together. How climate doesn't care about
lines on maps. How you, at the banks
of one river, are still so entangled with the
depths of another. How, if you've found
this poem, it's because you went off track.

Out of respect for Ruth, you go out and see if you can find this grave site. The map is poorly drawn and unlabeled. You could be walking toward anything.

Behind the church there are leaves and wind. Then there are ferns, and then the ferns break away. You stand at the mouth of a green tunnel made by the people who have walked this trail before you. You see moss growing on a solitary stone in the distance.

As you walk toward the stone, the leaves bend toward you like wanting hands. Finally, you kneel at the stone and brush away the moss. Strangely, you get the feeling that you will see your own name on the headstone, but you don't.

You don't see any name at all. It's just a rock.

Turn to page 90.

You feel like you can't deal with poetry anymore. At least not now. Recently, poetry has become a performance of grief for you. You stand up in front of people and recite all the worst things that have happened to you. Then those people clap. Your job is to make a pretty, efficient grief. To make memorable the things you want to forget.

Worse if it is nonfiction that wants to eat you whole. Or fiction with its audience demanding that you pull epiphany out of the mud.

You feel like you just can't afford all that.

But mostly you are tired of how poorly the categories fit. Part of you wants something else—a hyphenated art for our hyphenated lives. You think you might write that phrase down in a book, but, in reality, you never would. People would roll their eyes.

Map in your back pocket, you ignore it and cross the road so you can get a better look at the river below. There are wooden boxes and flowers on top of the cliff. And there are bees in those boxes. The flowers are mānuka. The bees are making flowers into food, flowers into medicine. You get close to one of the wooden boxes and wonder if the flurry of bee wings will make it vibrate.

Part of you wants to tell these bees about the bees in Costa Rica. But you don't. You don't want to scare the purposeful little pollinators. You don't want to push them into their dances of alarm.

You go back into the church and immediately hear a strange, cut-into-your-bones sound.

If you follow your first instinct and run away, turn to page—

but no, really, you can't. It could be Ruth. With family, you have no choice.

Down a short hall and left into a little decorated chapel. When you storm through the door, a short woman is looking at you with wide eyes.

But the woman is silent. There is a large cross on the wall, a little alcove of stained glass, a small altar. And under it all, Ruth is on her belly making the otherworldly sound.

A deep, luxurious noise, a scramble of not quite music, of not quite words. Ruth's muscular, brassy tone reverberates up to the high ceiling. You don't know what it means.

It is not distress; it is spiritual. But you don't know this immediately. You've lost the ability to tell the difference between emergency and epiphany.

When Ruth gets up on one knee, she takes your hand as help. She dusts off her dress and says calmly that sometimes it just comes over her. She doesn't say what *it* is, though. But it's clear that Ruth is fine. So fine that she doesn't even need to insist that she's fine.

You look at the woman there with Ruth and assume that she might be as surprised as you are. But that's not the look on her face. Tears are making little rivers down the woman's cheeks.

Things calm down. After some conversation with the stranger, you find out that she is on a journey of her own. She's getting married soon, and this trip down the river is one last self-exploration before she ties herself to someone else. She's been hiking for days and will finish off the trip by kayaking the river. You think that this is what *you* should be doing. You think you are on no kind of pilgrimage compared to her.

As if all her choices lead only to salvation.
As if all your choices lead only to ruin.

You fall so easily into this trap. If you are not doing it perfectly, then you are doing nothing. This way of thinking that stops us all from changing both ourselves and the world.

The woman talks about her fiancée in Christchurch. How she's down there right now rebuilding her family's villa all these years after the earthquake. With her own hands.

"And I'm just on this tiki tour."

Hearing this woman undercut her extraordinary trip, you start to understand what the "tall poppy" idea is all about. You understand how you do it yourself.

You look at Ruth for confirmation and are surprised that she has managed to produce three mugs from who knows where. Then the three of you sit, talking, blowing the hot off your tea.

Eventually, the caretaker comes and the woman has to sign papers for her stay. She hugs Ruth deeply before she leaves, says how *meaningful* their experience in the little chapel was. The woman is almost out of the room when she catches herself. She makes her choice to come back and ask Ruth if she would be free to officiate her wedding. Ruth has mentioned that this is something that she does, so it's not a strange request. Not strange but still surprising.

Ruth looks for a piece of paper to write down the woman's email address. There is nothing around except for the back of your useless little map.

You get back on the long road. When you finally stop, it's in Whanganui itself, the harbor town named after the river. It turns out that you are staying with Lula, one of Ruth's friends. They talk to each other over dinner in that lovely way that women who've known each other a long time talk. Different than simple sisterhood, they bear witness.

The joke in New Zealand is that the population is so small that everyone knows everyone. This is unfair. But when Ruth tells Lula why you are so interested in the river and its personhood, Lula says that she knows one of the people who helped with the legal work. In fact, he only lives a few streets away. Before you can say anything, she dials him, speaks for a minute, and then hands the phone to you.

An older man's voice says to come over. He says to bring a thumb drive. But he doesn't say where his house is.

You go alone and without Ruth beside you, the gentle guidance has gone quiet. And so you, like the whole town, reorient around the river. When Lula gives directions to the man's house, the Whanganui River is the only landmark she thinks to use.

When the man opens his front door, you are wary, not wanting to impose. But he says that he and Lula are whānau. And so any friend of hers . . . he finishes the sentence by welcoming you in.

The man is either a lawyer or someone used to dealing with lawyers. He uses words that are so precise that they are beyond you. But he's interested that you're interested, and so he speaks slowly. How do you turn a Māori worldview into a Western law, when the Western conception of law is part of what goes against that worldview? There are so many files to look at.

You explain about the citizen butterflies in Costa Rica. You talk about the bees and the trees. But in comparison to all his work, you feel sheepish. You tell him that it's nothing like what he's been doing. "It was more of a gesture, I think—greenwashing, even."

The man puts his hand up to stop you from tall poppying yourself. "Be careful," he says. "People don't believe in ideas. They believe in *people* who believe in ideas."

The man has read the same articles from around the world that you have. You talk for a long time about the people in Ecuador who've enshrined the rights of nature in their constitution. He gives you many examples that you didn't know about. A world of rights for mountains, rivers, and flora and fauna.

"But," he says, "a lot of that work is about climate change."

It's important that you understand that his work is *not* about climate change. It might be something that can address climate change, but it is not about it. It's about preserving beliefs in the face of a system built to break apart those beliefs. Beliefs that beat in the hearts of humans for hundreds of years before climate change.

The man is so patient. He walks you through what parts of the law he can. Sometimes you struggle with what it all means. The man smiles and tells you that no one has a problem thinking about what Air New Zealand *means*, what Woolworths *means*, or McDonald's.

You nod, but you don't understand. He explains how most of the world has already long agreed to open up personhood. We've opened it up to what we call "corporations"—now considered people in a legal context. "It's not such a strange idea," he says. "It's only strange when we do it for something other than a bottom line." As you are about to leave, he copies hundreds of files over to the thumb drive he asked you to bring along.

You hold years of the man's life in your palm. The word *corporeal*, then the word *corporation*, rolls on your tongue like a steel ball.

The next day, Ruth finally drives you down to the river. But before you get there, she turns to park in a little gravel lot. You can see the Whanganui flowing just over a field. The wind is blowing off the water toward you so hard that you can feel it inflating your lungs.

Ruth tells you that she wants to see somebody before visiting the river. She asks, do you want to go on one final errand and see this person?

If you follow Ruth one last time, turn the page.
If you still think this is only about you, turn back to page 73.

"OK," you say. You've gotten so used to following Ruth that you don't even ask who you are going to see.

Still, you are surprised when it turns out that the person Ruth wants to see is in the cemetery.

You follow Ruth down a well-kept path lined by a rustic wooden fence that leads away from the river. You are running your hand over the railing, and so you get a little splinter. This new pain reminds you of how the burn on your neck from the seat belt yesterday barely hurts anymore. Oh, so you can heal.

Ruth rummages in her purse for a safety pin so you can dig the splinter out of your palm. That's when she says that the grave you are going to visit belongs to her mother.

No, you think, it can't happen this way.

But with Ruth, the world is sudden ceremony. With Ruth, you can show up at an impromptu wake still trying to dig a splinter out of your hand.

First the little grave is cleaned, which means Ruth bending fully in half to pull at the weeds that rise around the headstone like a Victorian's collar.

Then Ruth sings a beautiful song. Then she pulls two wrapped sugar-free candies out of her pocket for you both to eat. Then the whole thing is over.

And now it's you who has tears making little rivers down your cheeks.

After Ruth is done, she thanks you for coming with her on her pilgrimage. She says that she'd wanted to do it for such a long time.

The directionality of the days is so clear now. *Her* directionality. The choices you've been half holding onto now fully fade. Of course, you were never really the hero of some choose-your-own-adventure tale. You are in the middle of Ruth's story, in the middle of her gift to you.

And that's when Ruth says it's time, points at the Whanganui, beautiful and wide.

You walk out alone, unsure what to do.

You are no expert in ceremony. Instead, you just sit by the river. You look up and the sky looks back at you.

On the banks of the long story of this extraordinary river you have nothing to give, and so you offer silence.

You think about your father, then you think about your mother. Then you think about nothing.

You have not been silent, truly silent, for such a long time.

Turn the page.

Just when you think your mind is blank, you notice a scrap of a song that has been knocking around your head. It's something that you've been carrying around with you this whole time, just below your consciousness. You try to sing along with it, hoping to dig the tune out of your memory. You close your eyes and concentrate and finally get its rhythm. Then you mouth a few of the words and laugh when it all comes.

So obvious, it's funny. This staple lullaby that your mother sang to you when you were young.

Los pollitos dicen
Pío, pío, pío
Cuando tienen hambre
Cuando tienen frío

You've never really thought about the meaning of those words. But now you really hear them. Hungry and cold. That's it—you've been thinking that you have nowhere to go when you are hungry and cold.

But there's more to it than that. Pío was your mother's nickname for you. Your mother is with you and she is not.

Pío, pío, pío.

You have one name, then two.
More than one thing can be true.

You open your eyes. Your name has come back. And there on the banks of the first river in the world to have legal personhood, you begin to feel like a whole person again.

Pío. If you were ever to tell the story of your life, you'd tell it in the third person, just so you could hear that name again.

The river is next to you, garrulous and wide. You thought that you had nothing to give. But you are wrong. You sit, you sing a little—for you, for the river. You try to step outside of yourself to find yourself, and you remember that you have a story to give.

V.

The Story

(Third Person)

It happened the day after the panther that was not a panther. Pío sat at his mother's kitchen table drinking rum out of a coffee cup. He frowned thinly to himself, listening to her bird sing from its wall-mounted cage. Flor's kitchen was a spongeable thing, bleach-splashed white counters, tiles that could take a cleaning. The house was cool white concrete, cracking from years of earthquake, but doing it slowly, almost politely.

Next to him, the back screen door opened out into his mother's patch of mango trees. He looked out at the green fruit pulling on the branches. In the distance, the dormant volcano stood tall. Its phosphorus-rich ash was what made all this land so fertile, for mangoes, for coffee, for people. This was what made this place livable, bankable. It was the town's mother mountain. Pío tried to spy the finca between the clouds.

The only exception to the hospital fitness of Flor's kitchen was the jilguero. No matter the situation, the little bird was always a mess—a seed kicker when it was happy, a newspaper shredder when it was sad. Costa Rican jilgueros are famous for their unnamable song. Imagine a glass harmonica and complicate it with radio static. Imagine the most *liquid* solid sound. Pío had spent the morning listening to the jilguero, drinking strong coffee, and hoping to pick up something of his mother in the bird's otherworldly music.

After a few cups, he hadn't liked how the coffee mimicked the symptoms of panic, so he'd started on a half bottle of rum he'd found in the cabinet. A twelve-year-old Flor de Caña, gorgeous Nicaraguan rum it hurt his pride to admit was better than whatever was coming out of the FANAL. Whoever'd brought the rum must have wanted to say, "I brought you a little piece of her." Pío's idea had been to smooth over his morning coffee, just a swallow of rum to silence his caffeine heart. But one traguito had become two, then three, and soon he'd felt himself tipping out of equilibrium.

So Pío was drowning in the kitchen chair when the smell of hortensias started wafting in from the next room. Somebody had gone up to the finca to bring back the sweet and sad blossoms. He knew that, given enough time, the flowers would take over every vase, every water glass and pot. Even his soon-to-be-empty bottle of rum. Pío tried again to distract himself with drink, but it tasted of hortensia.

In the living room, a rosary was starting, one of many in the days after the burial. The whole town was invited to this one, people coming in and out of the house. A wake was not about the dead person, Pío knew that. What was happening in the next room was about the family, the neighbors, the town. All the people who shared memories, all the people who lived in the shadow of the mountain. But after so long, he didn't want to be one of the people who remembered. He didn't want to be one of the living in the living room. What he wanted was a little more rum, and maybe a cigarette, and maybe a walk outside. Was it possible to lose yourself completely inside of rum and mango trees? Has anyone ever tried?

The open screen door tapped against its frame. Little bits of ripped up newspaper dropped from the birdcage in floating arcs. When Pío's aunt called his name to come and pray the rosary, only the jilguero was there to answer her call.

• • •

Pío couldn't see him through the curtain of backyard trees, but he knew his cousin was in there somewhere. The smell of Santi's cigar gave him away. He'd let Pío have a puff. He wouldn't make him talk about her. Santi was out by the river on the far side of the trees. He had a piece of fruit in his left hand and a skinny cigar in his right. He was wearing his usual boots and jeans but had added a black cowboy hat as a literal nod to mourning. When Pío walked up, Santi didn't greet him. Instead, he handed Pío his lit cigar and they picked up on an old conversation.

"I think you're right," Santi said, "that there aren't as many mangoes around here as when we were kids."

"Yeah," Pío said. He'd made this observation a week before, maybe two.

This jumping right back into an old conversation was the signature of Santi's love. When Pío had started going back and forth between the States and Costa Rica as a kid, he'd had trouble. Fumbling catch-ups, awkward reintroductions, the isolation of losing rhythm with your own family. But Santi wouldn't have it. He resolved to never worry about the gap between them. If Pío was in the States for a semester or at the beach for a week, Santi always treated him like he'd never left. Pío loved his cousin deeply for this.

"See, some bird has pecked this green one here," he said of a little mango. "That's proof. Birds only go for green fruit when there are no ripe ones left. And less ripe fruit means less fruit overall." Santi liked understanding how things were put together; he liked cause and effect. It was his mechanic's mind: a gear moved because another gear had affected it, and all of it could be traced back to some original combustion.

Pío took the pecked green fruit from Santi. A tangible, hold-it-in-your-hand proof that the climate was changing. Pío tried to think of something to say about mangoes. All that came to him was an old story about trying to buy green mangoes in a small town in Oklahoma. Pío couldn't find them anywhere, the grocers looking at him like he was crazy. Mangoes were bad enough, but unripe mangoes? Green?

The story was a gift for Santi in exchange for the little cigar. As a kid, Pío had brought back music from the States, TV shows taped off cable, and clothes and toys, and there'd been no doubt then which country was the one that had everything. It was nice, in the boys' eyes, for Costa Rica to have a little green something. Pío passed the cigar back to his cousin, whose puffing burned up a good minute.

Finally, Santi spoke again, gesturing now with the cigar. "I love that first bite. With a little salt and lime? That just grabs me, you know?"

Pío did know, and for a moment they were just two young men thinking about their mango-heavy childhoods. They were just cousins, no rosary happening inside the house, no crowd of mourners gathering in their dark clothes.

"You don't have to go in, you know," Santi said, looking at the house. He told Pío that they could walk down to the river instead. They could get out. They'd done this once as kids, pulled on rubber boots and walked the river's shallows for kilometers. It had happened years before. When Santi's own mother had died.

• • •

It was the eighties. Same house. More mangoes. After a long struggle, Santi's mother had died from the hole that had been growing in her body. Soon after it happened, a huge thirty-second earthquake rumbled her bed, rumbled the whole town. The coincidence was too much for little Santi, and he was convinced that the earthquake meant something, that the temblor must have been a sign, or better yet, the effect of his mother's spirit ripping away from this world.

It was a nice thought at first, a child's way of making sense of what cannot be made sense of. But after a few days, Santi was still tugging on the adults' shirts, telling them that they needed to help him find out more about the earthquake. Please do *something*. He begged Flor, who was so tired from nursing his mother that she could hardly move. The other adults just didn't listen. They told Santi to try to cry, to forget the earthquake, to focus on *what's really going on*. More than anything, they pushed rosaries into his hand. They hugged him in that way that adults do, confusing pity for love.

"Listen," little Santi said, pulling his cousin into a bedroom. His tone was hushed, conspiratorial.

When Pío heard Santi outline the mystery, he was surprised to see how far Santi had developed his personal mythology.

Santi put the pieces together for Pío: If the earthquake was his mother's soul leaving the world, then what did it leave behind for him? The earthquake would have left *something*. "Doesn't that make sense?"

Santi was two years older than Pío, a difference that meant everything at that age, and so Pío told his cousin that, yes, it did make sense. Pío kept finding himself saying *yes* that day. Yes, he understood. Yes, they should pack a bag. Yes, they should hike out to the epicenter and find what the earthquake, or Santi's mother, had left for him.

And so the two boys built provisions—a backpack for Pío to carry, some food, rubber boots, a little bent machete that their grandfather used to cut grass—and started scouting out to the epicenter.

They walked down the banks of the river that ran behind the house. They were looking for a long time before Pío realized that he wasn't sure what they were looking for. There was nothing out of the ordinary. Eventually, Santi couldn't hide his disappointment that there was no evidence of the earthquake, much less any evidence of something supernatural. The boys were young; they still thought that rupture had to be visible from the outside.

For Santi's sake, Pío tried hard to see things that weren't there. "Is that it?" Pío asked, pointing at a small hillock or fallen branch. "What about that?" No matter how much they tried, the two boys found nothing. Eventually the boys realized that they'd explored everything but the river itself. It could wet your ankle, but your waist was safe unless the rainy season had been particularly bad. To live on the banks of a river but not be able to swim, it was their first childhood injustice. Still, the boys were careful when they walked through the water, their boots pulled by the mud's suction.

An hour of hard river walking passed, and still there was nothing to find. Little Santi started to get angry, first at the river itself and then at Pío. He told Pío that the whole thing was *his fault*, that Pío was ruining everything. They couldn't find whatever it was they were looking for as long as he was around. Pío was too different now. He was too EE.UU. now, and it was scaring the sacred thing away.

Santi ordered Pío to go home, and when he didn't, Santi threatened him with a handful of rocky mud. Still, Pío didn't go. Some of it was love for Santi, but mostly it was fear. Not for himself; Pío was scared to leave Santi alone. Seeing the rocks in Santi's hands, Pío finally understood that something had broken in Santi's brain. The adults were right, Santi should be at home, crying into his rosary. Adults know how grief gets done.

So Pío followed his cousin from a distance. He walked along the banks and watched his cousin walk back and forth across the ribbon of river that shined just so in the noonday sun.

It took a long time before Santi stopped in the water. But it did happen.

When he stopped, he yelled for his cousin, "I found it!"

Pío ran. He had no idea what Santi had found, but this just made him run faster. He tried to keep an eye on Santi as he made his way, but the changing angle intensified the sun's glare on the water and Pío lost sight of his cousin. Then Pío heard Santi yell again and he tried to run toward the sound.

Moving fast, Pío scanned the horizon with a hand shading his eyes, but he couldn't find his cousin anywhere. That's when he realized that it wasn't just the glare; Santi had disappeared completely. This was the first time that Pío truly felt panic in his body.

But after a minute, Santi popped out from under the water and started dog-paddling. He was smiling! Pío couldn't believe it, but Santi had found *deep water*. Pío heaved off his backpack and started running again toward his cousin. He was so excited that he tripped. Pío scraped his face on the rocky riverbed, but it barely mattered. Little Pío got up, took off his shirt and boots, and kept on going.

It was hard to run through water and Pío ended up on his stomach again. That's when he went full sea turtle, pushing out into the middle of the river on his belly. Pío kicked and kicked, and then, in a beautiful instant, the water became deep enough to swim.

Pío leaned into it, freestyling now. He saw Santi trying to say something, but his voice was muted by splash. "No . . ." Santi kept saying, ". . . not . . .," ". . . spr . . . ." Pío dove deeper so he could swim faster.

Under the water, the world died down. It was quiet. Pío kicked his legs so hard that a ball of cramp developed in his calf. He couldn't swim anymore. That's when it came to him. That's when he realized that he'd gotten it all wrong. The deep water, that's not what Santi had found.

It came first as a sting on Pío's scraped face, then a mineral taste. Finally, Pío was completely enveloped by a rush of warm water. He did nothing. All of him unwound. He did less than nothing and let his body hang suspended in the amniotic heat. It was the only perfect moment of his entire life.

Pío came up for breath, splashed, yelled with a child's knowing joy what Santi already knew: "It's a hot spring!"

Santi and Pío played and wrestled there in the place that the earthquake had cracked open in the riverbed. Pío dunked Santi, and Santi dunked him. Eventually, Santi allowed himself to cry a little. Pío knew he did, even though the earth-warmed water hid his tears.

Pío hugged his cousin, their four feet kicking under the water. The volcanic mountain sat in the distance. Right then, Santi resolved to never let his cousin drift away. Right then, the two boys were linked forever. And in a single ecstatic scream they thanked the river in unison, they thanked God, and they thanked Santi's mother for remembering them on her way out of this world.

• • •

That was the rivery salvation that Santi, cigar in hand, was offering Pío underneath the mango trees. "Or I'll follow you back inside," he said. "Your choice."

Codas

First Person Plural I

for mother nature

Mere walking kicks up whole colonies,
clicks of bugs that chuck themselves

out of the grass like gentle fireworks.
A skinny apparatus of fur streaks by,

a rabbit, a blur that causes me to jump
back and almost fall. I walk down the hill

until the bushes blossom—tongues
of leaves that are all chlorophyll,

bees whirring with energy. Finally, I make it
to the river I love. I tell it where I've been.

We sit with each other for hours
and we gossip. We sluice, foam, and flow.

And because we are trying to make
connection and not meaning,

I end up saying a few truths into the blues
and greens. I, too, am wild and real.

First Person Plural II

for her motherland

Outside, near the wood pile
on the farm, there are bones.
An arranged scrap that looks
so meticulous I assume it's there
for me, that some animal has spent
the night spelling out words
in a language older than words.
I show my cousin this rotting prophecy,
and he's immediately worried.
Not because of the future and its nest
of threats but because he thinks
the neighbor's coop is open.

On our way to check on the chickens
we hunt through the fields for fugitive
culantro, shovel up a row of our
infant potatoes. We disturb the little
nation of hanging chayotes. When we
pass our neighbor's corrugated pigsty,
I am suddenly eye to eye with a sow.
I keep my distance, her flank radiating
heat from meters away.

The neighbor's chickens are plentiful
and accounted for as they weave through
my legs and peck at my boot tops.
Later, we cousins cook our vegetables
with a packet of Maggi, and I think about
the accidents of proximity, how I see
myself in a story of losing this place.

My cousin, now fully living in the city,
laughs and says I am not the first person
to feel this. We eat, we drink, we cry.
When we are finished, we clean out the pot.

I am of this place and not of this place,
and that is OK. Somewhere, the glorious
sow is sleeping, her legs stretched out
from her body. Her dreams are not
of just one thing.

First Person Plural III

for my mother

I return and the asphalt breaks around
my footsteps as I get off the bus and say
only two words to the local taxista,
Flor and *Argüello*, my mother's name.
This is why I don't use Uber, to have
this proof that someone still knows her,
that we share a past in common.
As he drives, the old town goes by,
the old river with its good years and bad,
the old shoulders of the old mountain
newly scarred with cuts of construction.
This has always been my life: leave and
regresar, salir y return. After my mother died,
I was afraid that burying her under
this volcanic ash meant that the center
had changed. Now I am back again
for a wedding. Not a funeral, not to talk
to lawyers about citizenships and cédulas.
When I arrive at the house, I tap
with a golden coin onto the wrought-iron bars
that cover our door and say, ¡Upe!,
but no one is there. The door is flounced
with crosses and growing curlicues
that are both beautiful and sad. Eventually,
I see two sets of eyes glinting with sun.
My mother's brindled boxers run up,
frame their faces in the window, and paw
at the glass. The dogs' high whines say,
We remember you, we remember you.
Not only does the center hold,
the center is all there is.

When my cousin opens the door,
we don't say any words. Instead, we
instantly wrap our arms tight around
each other's shoulders, as the two gorgeous
dogs guau guau their song of unforgetting
and show us their endless tongues.

Acknowledgments

Poem-a-Day by the Academy of American Poets: "The Name of Grasses" (titled "Outside in Oklahoma" in this collection), January 2026.

Poetry Magazine: "The Change in Climate Change," 2023.

EcoTheo Review: "Not Yet" and "The Return," 2023.

What Things Cost Anthology: An Anthology for the People: "Behind You," 2023.

Oxford American Magazine: "Grief," "Grief," and "Goose" (titled "Grief, Grief, Goose" in this collection), 2022.

Oxford American Magazine: "Flashlight," Spring 2021.

Border Lines: Poems of Migration (Everyman's Library Pocket Poets Series): "Workshop," October 2020.

Epiphany Magazine: "Crossing Over 1" and "Crossing Over 2," Spring/Summer 2019.

The Slowdown (podcast and radio show) from American Public Media: "Workshop," October 2019.

Poem-a-Day by the Academy of American Poets. "Workshop," September 2018.

• • •

My deep gratitude to the fellowships and institutions whose support made this work possible: the American Academy in Rome, Bread Loaf Writers' Conference, Yaddo, the Hodder Fellowship at Princeton University, Baylor University, the Jack Kerouac Writers in Residence Project, Sewanee Writers' Conference, and the Lannan Foundation.

For their generosity and insight, thank you to Rebecca Gayle Howell, G. A. Chaves, Taneum Bambrick, Eduardo C. Corral, Wesley Rothman, and A. Van Jordan.

Thank you to University of Arizona Press, and especially to Rigoberto [illegible] and Elizabeth Wilder, whose editorial care and vision shaped these pages.

To Jane Chester, without whose remarkable spirit this book would not have entered the world.

And to Chloe Honum, for every step of the way.

About the Author

Jacob Shores-Argüello is a Costa Rican American poet and prose writer. His second book, *Paraíso,* was selected for the inaugural CantoMundo Poetry Prize. He is a 2018–19 Hodder Fellow at Princeton University, a Lannan Literary Fellow for Poetry, a 2024–25 Rome Prize winner in literature, and a 2026–27 Radcliffe Fellow at Harvard University. His poetry and fiction has appeared in *The New Yorker*, *Poetry Magazine*, *Poem-a-Day* by the Academy of American Poets, and *The Oxford American*, among other publications. His work examines borders—between geologies, cultures, and languages, and between humanity and the natural world.